THE BIPOLAR DISORDER JOURNAL

Guided Prompts to Help You Understand, Track, and Manage Your Symptoms

Whitney Frost, LPC, MA

Interior and Cover Designer: Gabe Nansen
Art Producer: Megan Baggott
Editor: Adrian Potts
Production Editor: Jenna Dutton
Production Manager: Holly Haydash

Published by Callisto Publishing LLC C/O Sourcebooks LLC
P.O. Box 4410, Naperville, Illinois 60567-4410
(630) 961-3900
callistopublishing.com

Printed in the United States of America.

The Bipolar Disorder Journal

CONTENTS

INTRODUCTION

Hello, and welcome to this journal. My name is Whitney Frost, and I'm a licensed professional counselor who specializes in treating bipolar disorder. Whether you have been recently diagnosed with bipolar disorder or have been in treatment for some time, you know the many challenges of living with the condition. Through this journal, you will find a space to better understand your moods, identify your triggers, and examine your coping strategies so you can live a more fulfilling life.

From when I was a clinical intern at the Jefferson Center for Mental Health through to my current practice, I have been passionate about helping those with bipolar disorder find relief from their symptoms and a greater sense of stability. I also have a close family member and many friends who live with bipolar 1 and 2. I know that society is often unkind and lacks awareness of the struggles people with this disorder face. My hope is that in using the prompts and practices in this journal, you can find a degree of freedom from the misunderstanding and stigma that a diagnosis can bring.

While journaling can be a hugely beneficial practice, it is important to note that this journal is not meant as a replacement for therapy or medication, and it should be used in conjunction with psychiatric services. The Resources section on page 124 includes useful information about finding the right help as you continue to gain more strength, confidence, and balance in your daily life.

A BRIEF OVERVIEW OF BIPOLAR DISORDER

Bipolar disorder is a psychiatric condition characterized by sometimes-drastic mood swings known as "episodes." These episodes can include depression, mania, or hypomania and can last weeks or months. (In the early 1900s, this disorder was referred to as "manic depression.") There's no set schedule for how a person with bipolar disorder moves through mood episodes; the length and cause of cycles vary.

The root cause of bipolar disorder still has not been discovered, but it is currently believed to be a combination of genetics, environment, and brain chemistry. The disorder often develops around the late teenage years or in early adulthood, although it can be diagnosed much later.

Bipolar 1 is diagnosed when a full manic episode has occurred at some point in someone's life. This can include a decreased need for sleep, irritability, an inflated sense of self or grandiosity, and impulsivity with drugs, sex, alcohol, spending, and other high-risk behaviors. Bipolar 2 is diagnosed when hypomania has occurred. Hypomania is a mild version of a manic episode, but it often occurs more frequently—referred to as "rapid cycling." Whether a person has bipolar 1 or bipolar 2, mania is typically followed by a depressive episode.

While there is no known cure for bipolar disorder, with the right treatment and coping skills, it is possible to manage the symptoms and enjoy a more balanced life.

HOW TO USE THIS JOURNAL

Throughout this journal, you will find a variety of writing prompts, practices, and exercises designed to help you better understand and manage your symptoms; they are based on several types of therapeutic theories and interventions. Each of the first five parts of the journal is focused on managing a different aspect of bipolar disorder:

- **Part 1: Understanding Manic Episodes**
- **Part 2: Navigating Depressive Episodes**
- **Part 3: Recognizing Your Triggers**
- **Part 4: Embracing Your Coping Skills**
- **Part 5: Establishing Healthy Relationships**

In part 6, you will find five two-week trackers, each of which correlates with a part of the journal. These are designed for you to track your moods, behaviors, and habits over time and to help you understand how the prompts, practices, and exercises are working for you. You can begin tracking at any point in the journal; you do not need to wait until the end. Feel free to use this journal in whatever way you find most beneficial.

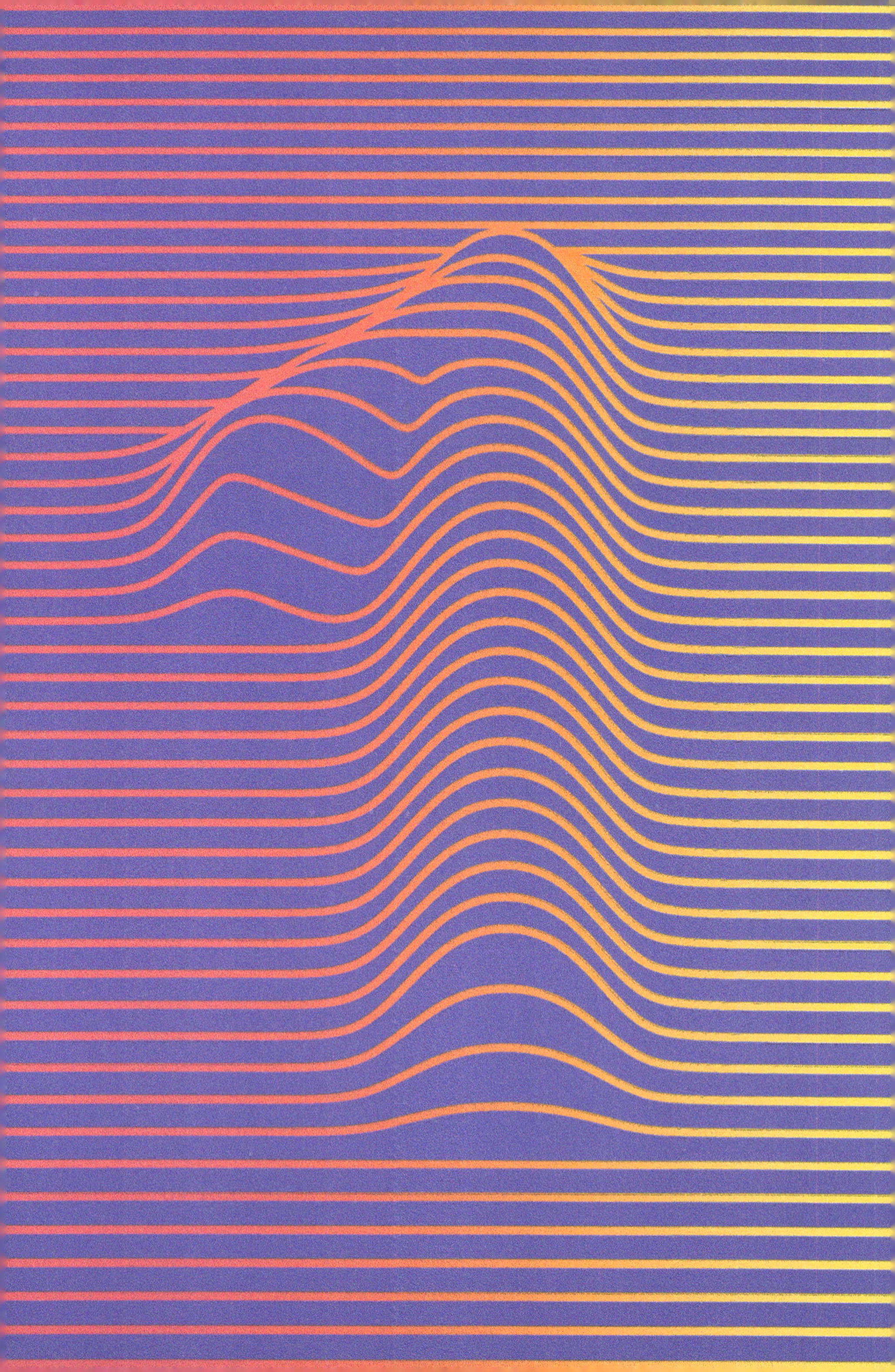

PART 1

Understanding Manic Episodes

Mania, or a manic episode, is a swift chemical change occurring within the brain that results in mood imbalances. Mania can look like euphoria, grandiosity, or feelings of being invincible or godlike, as well as impulsivity or rage.

Extreme life stressors, illness, medication side effects, underlying medical conditions, and lack of sleep can all trigger manic episodes. Traumatic brain injuries, encephalitis, brain tumors, dementia, medication, childbirth, and acute high levels of stress can also trigger manic episodes without the diagnosis of bipolar disorder.

We will look more at your triggers in part 3, but in this part, you will have a chance to reflect on your experience with manic episodes and how to better navigate the thoughts and feelings that accompany them.

Your Experience with Mania

Distinguishing the symptoms of mania from general irritability and grumpiness can be difficult, but it will be immensely beneficial in predicting and preparing for the onset of a manic episode. When you start to feel irritable or grumpy, you may be afraid of experiencing a manic episode. Use the checklist here to help identify which symptoms of mania are most common for you during an episode.

- ☐ Decreased sleep for more than three nights
- ☐ Irritability and/or agitation
- ☐ Impulsiveness with spending, sex, speeding, alcohol use; general reckless behavior
- ☐ Euphoria or feelings of elation and excitement for no reason
- ☐ Increased sense of self-esteem without a reason
- ☐ Racing thoughts
- ☐ Rapid speech

Use this space to write about any other symptoms that are common for you.

Your History with Mania

When did you first notice your manic episodes? What was going on in your life when they started? Were you experiencing a time of high stress? Were you experiencing a severe illness? Were you using drugs or alcohol?

Label Your Feelings

Take a moment, away from any distractions, to get comfortable in a seated position. Take a few deep breaths in through your nose and out through your mouth. Notice your thoughts come in and out of your mind. What feelings do you notice? Label the feelings as they enter and leave your mind. Do not place any judgment on these feelings; simply label them to bring awareness to them. Feelings are not good or bad, positive or negative. Feelings are just feelings. Try this activity for five minutes.

What feelings did you notice? Was it hard for you to label your feelings? Was it difficult not to judge your feelings? What feelings are the most prevalent for you? What did it feel like to do this activity? What did you discover?

Pros and Cons of Engaging in Impulsive Behavior

It's not uncommon to engage in high-risk, impulsive behaviors during manic episodes. These behaviors can include speeding, drug use, promiscuous sex, spending money you don't have, or dangerous, even criminal behaviors. Behaviors like these can interfere with your short-term and long-term goals for your life and your relationships and be out of alignment with your values and morals. Think about three impulsive behaviors you tend to repeat during manic episodes. Use the space provided to name each impuslive behavior and make a list of the pros and cons of acting on the impulses versus resisting them. Take a picture of your list or keep it with you to help reinforce the decisions you make when you are feeling impulsive.

IMPULSE 1: ______________________

	ACTING ON IMPULSE 1	RESISTING IMPULSE 1
PROS		
CONS		

continues >

IMPULSE 2: ______________________

	ACTING ON IMPULSE 2	RESISTING IMPULSE 2
PROS		
CONS		

IMPULSE 3: ______________________

	ACTING ON IMPULSE 3	RESISTING IMPULSE 3
PROS		
CONS		

TIPP Skill

The TIPP skill is a super-easy skill to help ground you during a manic episode. It was created by Marsha M. Linehan in her dialectical behavior therapy (DBT) work. The acronym stands for:

Tip the temperature

Intense exercise

Paced breathing

Paired muscle relaxation

Combining these skills, or even using one of the skills on its own, can reduce your feelings of being highly emotional and help you avoid acting impulsively or destructively when you are not processing information correctly, when you are having an emotional crisis, or when you are too overwhelmed to make a decision.

Tip the temperature: Fill a large bowl with ice water, hold your breath, and stick your face in the bowl for thirty seconds. (Do not attempt this if you have any cardiac problems!)

Intense exercise: Raise your heart rate for fifteen to thirty minutes with exercise. Run in place, do jumping jacks, play basketball, go for a jog, go for a swim, or ride your bike.

continues >

Paced breathing: Try to slow your breathing down to five or six breaths per minute. This means one complete breath cycle of inhaling and exhaling should take ten to twelve seconds.

Paired muscle relaxation: Practice tensing your muscles as you breathe in for five or six seconds. Notice how you feel. Then relax them as you breathe out, paying attention to how that feels as you do it. Notice the difference between the feeling of tension and the feeling of relaxation. Go through each muscle group in the body (follow the list provided) and tense and then relax each one. As you relax each muscle group, say to yourself, "Relax."

1. Toes
2. Feet
3. Heels
4. Ankles
5. Calves
6. Thighs
7. Buttocks
8. Hips
9. Stomach
10. Abdominals
11. Chest
12. Biceps
13. Triceps
14. Wrists
15. Hands
16. Fingers
17. Neck
18. Cheeks
19. Mouth
20. Eyes
21. Forehead
22. Crown of the head

Calming the Chaos around You

During manic episodes, it's not uncommon to find yourself with a lot of energy but getting nothing accomplished—metaphorically walking in circles. Creating a calm environment or organizing your environment to at least manage the chaos can help reduce your anxiety and stress. Try organizing just one room a day. Put away every item that's out of place until, in a few days, every room in your home is tidy and everything is where it should be. Don't forget the dirty dishes; making the bed; washing, folding, and putting away the laundry; and showering yourself.

What Mania Looks Like for You

The symptoms of bipolar disorder and mania differ from one person to the next. How do your manic episodes commonly present? (The trackers on pages 112 and 113 will help you check in with your symptoms.) Have your symptoms changed over time?

Releasing Shame

Thinking back on your current or most recent manic episode, what are some feelings or actions that bring up feelings of shame for you? What about these feelings or actions causes you shame? Rather than blaming yourself, how would it feel to be more compassionate with yourself about your past behavior, knowing the role bipolar disorder plays in your actions?

Making Peace

Mania can be destabilizing in many ways, but it can also be freeing to reflect on how your history has helped you grow into who you are today. Take some time to write about what you have learned from your mania. While acknowledging the difficulties mania brings, are there any positives that have come from it?

Playing Out the Script

Before engaging in an activity or behavior that could have negative consequences, stop and play out the script all the way to the end. Think ahead, as if you are watching a movie of yourself, and consider all the possible consequences of your actions before you engage. Do you like the end of this movie? Can you afford the possible consequences of your behavior? Are there legal ramifications? Will you or a loved one end up hurt emotionally or physically? Is the temporary high or thrill worth the long-term effects? How would this behavior interfere with your short-term and long-term goals?

Establish Your Routine

During a manic episode, it can feel as if your life is out of control. You can find some stability within the chaos by setting up and sticking to a daily routine. Make a list of the most important things you need to do each day to make your life functional. Assign a time for each activity. Set reminders in your cell phone (or whatever reminder system works well for you) to alert you that you need to complete the activity. Some of these activities might be daily (for example, feed my cat, eat lunch, take my medication), and some might be less often (such as pay the rent, wash my hair).

DAY(S)	TIME	ACTIVITY

Unpacking Your Thoughts

"Cognitive distortions" are habitual ways of thinking that are often inaccurate and biased toward negativity—that life sucks, people don't care about you, or things aren't worth doing. Some common cognitive distortions are all-or-nothing thinking (it's all totally good or totally bad), overgeneralizing (assuming you know what's going to happen all the time based on one event), jumping to conclusions (mind reading or fortune-telling), disqualifying the positive (discounting the positive things that have happened), and personalizing (blaming yourself). During manic episodes, cognitive distortions can lead to impulsive behaviors such as self-harm, reckless behavior, and behavior that damages relationships.

What are some cognitive distortions you tend to engage in when you are in a manic episode? How do these cognitive distortions affect you and those around you? Write down some of the cognitive distortions you tell yourself, and then write what the opposite would be. For example, "I am a bad person because of my mental illness." Opposite: "I am capable and worthy of love and kindness."

Check the Facts before You Act

How you perceive a situation—especially during a manic episode, when you do not always see things clearly—can lead to a misunderstanding of what's really happening and an emotional response that doesn't actually fit with the facts. Check the Facts, a skill created by dialectical behavior therapy (DBT) founder Marsha M. Linehan, can be a great skill to help sort out facts from perceptions.

Think back to a recent situation where you experienced cognitive distortions that were not based in fact. How could checking the facts improve or change the situation? How could it affect your feelings about the situation and improve the outcome?

Freeze before You Speak

The next time you are feeling angry or about to engage in a conversation that you might regret later, come to this page and write down all the things you want to say here. Then return to the page in thirty minutes and see if you still feel the same way or if the urge or feeling has passed. Repeat this two or more times or until you notice the anger or rage fade away. Do not engage in the conversation until you notice that your level of anger has reduced.

Get Your Thoughts Down

Often, it can be difficult to compose your thoughts during a manic episode because your thoughts are racing and feel like they're coming at you like a speeding train. When you experience mania, take a moment to write down your thoughts here, even if they don't make sense or don't seem logical. Sometimes when we write down our thoughts instead of allowing them to spiral in our head, it allows us to find peace and clarity, to breathe, and to find some room to think.

Physical Sensations

When you're having a manic episode, how do you notice it present within your body? Do you feel physical sensations along with mental ones?

Knowing When to Ask for Help

Mania or manic episodes are not always dangerous and do not always lead to problematic outcomes, but they do have the potential to escalate to danger for you and those around you. What are the signs that your manic episodes are escalating and it's time to ask for help from a loved one or a professional? List them here. How have you learned over time when you need to ask for help? Who are your supports? (The Resources section on page 124 contains information about seeking help.)

PART 2

Navigating Depressive Episodes

Depressive episodes, or "lows," are when you experience loss of interest, low energy, flat affect (not expressing emotions), tearfulness, fatigue, social isolation, lack of motivation, thoughts of suicide, feelings of hopelessness or worthlessness, lack of pleasure, feelings of guilt, and/or feelings of discontent. These depressive lows typically follow a manic episode, but they can occur on their own. Depressive episodes can last a week or longer. The symptoms can make it difficult to go to school or work and complete the activities of daily life, such as showering, eating, getting out of bed, and socializing.

Managing your stress, diet, and daily habits, and taking your medication as prescribed are the standard recommendations for managing depressive episodes, but they can still occur even when you do everything "right." So the goal is to reduce their occurrence and severity. In this chapter, you will explore prompts, activities, and practices to help guide your understanding of depressive episodes and manage the symptoms associated with them.

Your Experience with Depression

Distinguishing the symptoms of depression from general sadness and lack of interest can be difficult, but it can also be very important in predicting and preparing for a depressive episode. When you start to feel uninterested or sad for more than two days, you may be afraid of experiencing a depressive episode. Use the checklist here to help identify which symptoms of depression are most common for you during an episode.

- ☐ Increased need for sleep for more than three nights
- ☐ Isolation from social activities
- ☐ Lack of interest in activities that normally bring you joy
- ☐ Loss of appetite or increased appetite
- ☐ Tearfulness
- ☐ Loss of joy
- ☐ Restlessness
- ☐ Irritability

Use this space to write about any other symptoms that are common for you.

Reflecting on Depression

When did you first notice your depressive episodes? How did depression first present in your life? How were those feelings different from how you feel today? Have you noticed that your depression changes throughout the year? In what ways?

continues >

Your Body

When you're having a depressive episode, how do you notice it present within your body? Do you feel physical sensations along with mental ones? Do you notice yourself becoming physically ill or experiencing an increase in pain?

Celebrating the Little Things

During a depressive episode, completing simple activities such as bathing or getting dressed can be reasons to celebrate. Make a list of small rewards for yourself that you would genuinely enjoy having when you are struggling, like a coffee at your favorite café or a bouquet of flowers. Make another list of activities you enjoy doing or that feel good; use them to remind yourself of things you can do that don't take a lot of energy and that will help you feel better when you are not feeling your best.

Rewards for myself

1.
2.
3.
4.
5.

Activities I enjoy

1.
2.
3.
4.
5.

Shine Some Light on It

During episodes of depression, it can be really helpful to sit outside for half an hour. A 2019 study from Harvard Medical School showed that at least thirty minutes of sunshine a day can help reduce feelings of depression. A 2020 follow-up study also from Harvard suggests that people who struggle with bipolar disorder can benefit from between thirty minutes and two hours of bright light a day during depressive episodes. So find a spot outside that you enjoy. Take a book, music, a snack, or a craft; or go for a stroll.

If you live in a dark or wintry climate, you may benefit from light therapy, in which you expose yourself to artificial light. So-called seasonal affective disorder (SAD) lamps can be easily purchased and used in your own home. These emit a special kind of light that replicates some of the beneficial effects of natural sunlight. Be sure to speak with a medical professional to decide if this may be suitable for you.

Ground Yourself

Often, we forget the power nature can have to uplift us. Find a place with some trees or other plants and some dirt or grass. Take off your shoes and put your feet in the dirt or on a patch of grass. (If it's too cold, you can still ground yourself in nature with your shoes on.) Plant yourself in the earth for fifteen to twenty minutes without any distractions from technology. Take in the energy from the natural world around you. Pay attention to the sounds you hear. Then notice what you feel: How does the grass or dirt feel? How does the earth feel beneath your feet? How does the air feel on your face? Take some deep breaths of the fresh air. Use this space to make any notes about your experience.

Affirm Yourself

Depression can lead to negative thought patterns and feelings of worthlessness and hopelessness. Think about some affirmations or positive statements about yourself that you can hold on to and continue to repeat throughout your periods of depression. Here are a few to get you going. Add your own in the lines that follow. When you are finished, write out a few affirmations on a sticky note or put them in your phone and read them to yourself or out loud every day.

- I add value to the world.
- I deserve good things.
- I cannot be replaced.
- I am capable of creating the life I want.
- I am worthy of love.

Avoid Avoiding

Sometimes the anticipation of an activity is worse than the activity itself. When you avoid avoiding—in other words, just jump in—it can help you get things done. What are some of the tasks or activities in your life that you avoid when you are depressed? How does your depression contribute to you avoiding these activities?

Is delaying these activities stopping you from reaching your short-term or long-term goals? How would completing these activities improve your life and help you feel more accomplished?

What are some action steps you could take this week to help you stop avoiding and just take action?

Finding Balance in Life

How much do you need to move, sleep, eat, and hydrate each day to meet your needs, manage your stress, and feel like the best version of yourself? Write down what you need. Then write about how you can fit that in with work, school, and your social life. Be as specific as you can. For example, "I need eight hours of sleep, so I need to make sure I go to bed no later than midnight every night since I have to be up at 8 a.m. for work every day."

Build Up Your Supports

Depression can feel isolating and lonely. It can be difficult to reach out to loved ones or ask for help when you're in the middle of a depressive episode, even when you know they are willing to help. Make a list of people you can depend on for support when things get difficult. You may choose the same or different people for each category—maybe a friend for one, a family member for another, your therapist for the next, and so on.

People I can call or text:

People I can tell how I'm really feeling:

People who will help me with chores:

People who will make me laugh:

People who will get me out of the house:

People who will check in on me daily:

Phone a Friend

It's easy to feel isolated and down during depressive episodes, allowing negative self-talk to creep in and tell you that you are not worthy or that no one likes you. Make a list of go-to people you can call when you're feeling down and just need to talk. Call those people and have a conversation with them about current events, how you're feeling, and/or what's new in their lives; or invite them over just to sit with you and keep you company.

Negative Thought Train

When you are not feeling worthy or when you are feeling hopeless, cognitive distortions can take over and seem like the truth. As you learned in part 1, some common cognitive distortions are all-or-nothing thinking (it's all totally good or totally bad), overgeneralizing (assuming you know what's going to happen all the time based on one event), jumping to conclusions (mind reading or fortune-telling), disqualifying the positive (discounting the positive things that have happened), and personalizing (blaming yourself).

What are some cognitive distortions you tend to engage in when you are feeling depressed? How do these cognitive distortions intensify your feelings of depression? Write down some of the cognitive distortions you tell yourself, and then write what the opposite would be. For example, "I am a terrible friend, and no one wants to spend time with me because of my depression." Opposite: "I care about my friends and am worthy of love and friendship despite my mental illness."

continues >

Activities of Daily Living List

When you're dealing with a depressive episode, it can be hard to do everyday activities. Think about the daily tasks in your life that can be difficult to complete when you experience a depressive episode. Make a list of the activities you do each day in a typical week to remind yourself to complete the basic activities of daily life (such as brushing your teeth, showering, and eating breakfast). When you're struggling, come back to this list to remind yourself what you need to accomplish.

DAYS	ACTIVITIES
MONDAY	
TUESDAY	
WEDNESDAY	
THURSDAY	
FRIDAY	
SATURDAY	
SUNDAY	

Remind Yourself of a Better Time

Hopelessness and doubt can be common themes associated with depressive episodes. Think about a time when things felt better, when you were doing better, or when you were accomplishing your goals and felt capable of doing hard things. Write out a story about that time to remind yourself that depressive episodes are temporary and that it's still possible to feel better.

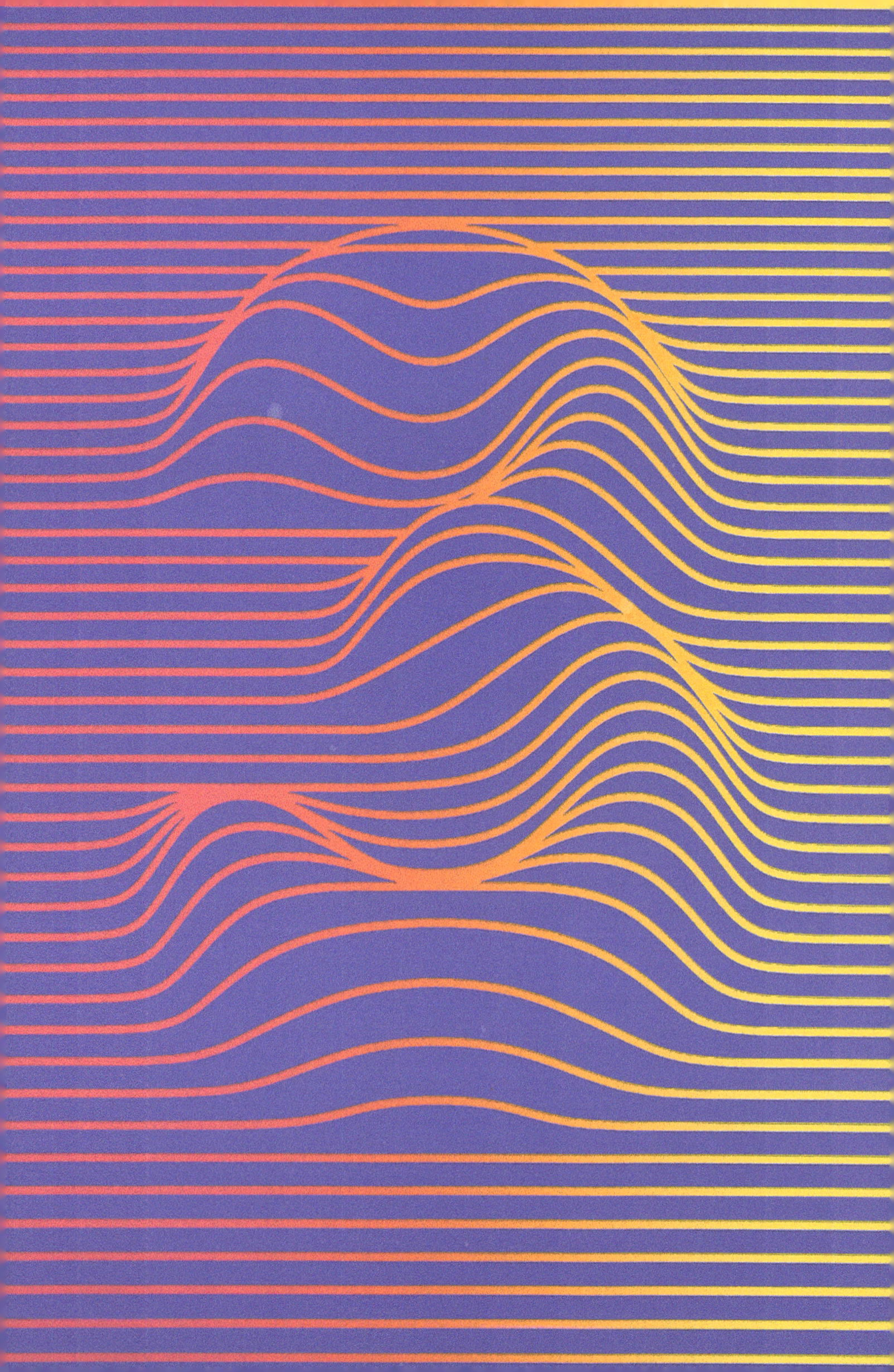

PART 3

Recognizing Your Triggers

At first, the mood episodes of bipolar disorder may take you by surprise. But over time, you will likely start to see patterns and signs of what triggers an episode for you, such as stress, poor sleep, the change of seasons, and other triggers. In this part, you will work on identifying what triggers are most common and challenging for you.

There are several benefits to becoming more familiar with your triggers. You will be able to figure out which ones you can avoid, better cope with those that are unavoidable or take you by surprise, and recognize when you are most vulnerable so you can get the treatment and support you need. This also lays the foundation for you to find the best routine and self-care practices to manage bipolar disorder throughout your life, which we'll explore more in part 4.

Common Triggers

Many lifestyle and environmental factors can contribute to or trigger a mood episode. The most common are listed here. Check those that apply to you and use the blank spaces to write about any others you have uncovered.

- ☐ **Poor sleep:** This includes a lack of sleep or sudden changes in sleep patterns, such as when you're traveling across time zones.
- ☐ **Stress:** Stressful life changes, such as the end of a relationship, losing a loved one, interpersonal conflict, the loss of a job, and financial pressure, can all be triggers for a mood episode.
- ☐ **Drug and alcohol use:** Using drugs and alcohol can disrupt the chemical balance of your brain and trigger a mood episode.
- ☐ **Medication changes:** Sometimes changes in your medications can trigger changes in mood.
- ☐ **Seasonal changes:** For some, the change of seasons can trigger mood swings. Winter is typically associated with depressive episodes, while spring and summer are more commonly linked with manic episodes.
- ☐ **Pregnancy and hormonal conditions:** Menstrual cycles, pregnancy, and the postpartum period can trigger manic or depressive episodes.
- ☐ **Other:**
- ☐ **Other:**
- ☐ **Other:**

Describing a Trigger

Pick a trigger from the previous exercise. If you could describe your trigger to someone, how would you describe it? What does it look like? How does it feel? What physical characteristics does it have? What emotional characteristics does it have? Is it big, or is it little? How did it become a trigger for you?

Reflecting on Your Experiences

Reflecting more on your triggers, think about what specific situations, events, life changes, actions, or people have been challenging for you in the past. Write about the most challenging ones and how they affected you.

Manic Triggers

Thinking back on previous manic episodes, can you recall specific triggers, such as events, substance use, or anything else that preceded them? How did these triggers influence your mood? How have these manic episodes affected the relationships in your life? How have they affected other areas of your life (legal, financial, social, emotional, and others)?

STOP Coping Skill

When you find yourself being triggered and unable to act from a place of thoughtfulness or mindfulness, try using the STOP skill. It is a skill used in dialectical behavior therapy (DBT), created by Marsha M. Linehan. It is best to use this skill when you feel as if your emotions are about to take over.

Stop: Physically freeze and do not move.

Take a step back: Remove yourself from the situation.

Observe what is going on: Notice what is going on for you physically and emotionally, as well as what is going on for others. Notice what you are thinking and feeling. Remember to gather facts, not perceptions.

Proceed mindfully: When you feel confident in your ability to proceed mindfully, continue with the activity.

Think of a situation in which you could use this skill and try rehearsing it in your mind.

Depressive Triggers

Thinking back on previous depressive episodes, can you identify any common triggers that have preceded them, such as lack of sleep, the change of seasons, or specific stressors? How did these triggers influence your mood? How have these depressive episodes affected the relationships in your life? How have they affected other areas of your life (legal, financial, social, emotional, and others)?

Your Triggers and Your Feelings

Thinking about some of your more common triggers, how do you feel when they occur? Do you feel angry, sad, scared, excited, or otherwise? What sensations occur when you experience a trigger? How do you respond to any feelings that arise?

Identifying the Trigger

Often when we feel triggered, we do not know the root cause of why we feel triggered and why we are experiencing the emotions that arise. In this exercise, you will practice naming the primary emotion that results from a triggering event. Think of specific examples from events in your past. I've provided an example to get you started.

Triggering event: *I was at a party that was very loud. I was talking to my partner, who turned away from me in the middle of our conversation and started talking to someone else.*
Emotional response: *I felt frustrated, unheard, and unimportant. This made me close off from my partner and resent them.*

Triggering event:

Emotional response:

Triggering event:

Emotional response:

Triggering event:

Emotional response:

Your Values

Your values are the guiding principles and priorities that you consider important in your life. When these are ignored, disrespected, or violated, it can trigger a strong emotional reaction that can destabilize your mood. Becoming clear about what your values are enables you to better pursue and protect them. Check the values you consider the most important.

- ☐ Achievement
- ☐ Balance
- ☐ Compassion
- ☐ Courage
- ☐ Empathy
- ☐ Faith/religion/spirituality
- ☐ Family
- ☐ Freedom
- ☐ Friendship
- ☐ Generosity
- ☐ Health
- ☐ Integrity
- ☐ Kindness
- ☐ Knowledge
- ☐ Love
- ☐ Peace
- ☐ Personal development
- ☐ Purpose
- ☐ Respect
- ☐ Stability
- ☐ Structure
- ☐ Togetherness
- ☐ Tradition
- ☐ Transparency

Use this space to write about any others.

A Valuable Reminder

Choose an important value that you selected from the previous page and write about how it has guided you in life. You can describe a specific time that honoring the value helped you in a situation. Or you might write more generally about how the value has helped you navigate the world.

The People in Your Life

Your relationships with your partner, family, friends, colleagues, and other people can greatly influence your mood. On the one hand, they can provide you with love and support; on the other, they can cause stress through conflict, disagreement, and other challenges. Write about the people in your life who trigger you. What do they do to trigger you? Why is that a trigger for you? What would you tell them about how they make you feel? What do you wish they would do differently?

When and Where

Are there certain places that you seem to experience triggers more than others? Are there certain times of the day, week, or year that you experience triggers more than others? What is it about those times that causes you more distress and increases your likelihood of being triggered?

Check the Facts

Many times, when people are triggered, they act from a place of emotional thinking and not from a place of mindfulness or logic. When you are acting from a place of emotion, you are more likely to be impulsive. In these instances, it is useful to return to the Check the Facts skill you first explored on page 18. This can be a helpful skill for managing your perceptions and leading with clarity and logic before acting. Remember, a fact is something that is known or has been proven to be true.

Bring to mind a situation in which you have been triggered in the past or may be in the future, and think through how you can follow these steps. Use the spaces provided to write down your thoughts.

1. Identify the emotion that was problematic.

2. Identify the situation that triggered the emotion.

3. Make a list of your assumptions about the situation. For example, were you assuming a threat or criticism?

4. Make a list of facts that you have about the situation. Stick to things that actually happened, with no added descriptions or judgments.

5. Do the facts fit your assumptions and your emotional response? If the facts do not fit, explore and problem-solve an appropriate emotional response that fits the facts.

Cope Ahead

Sometimes you just can't avoid triggering events or people. For these triggers, it's helpful to practice the Cope Ahead skill—planning for the situation and writing out a script. This skill from dialectical behavior therapy (DBT) can help you feel calmer and more in control of your responses.

First, imagine the worst-case scenario of the triggering event or task and how you might feel in that scenario. What is happening? How does it feel?

Now plan and write out a script for how you would like to move through the worst-case scenario, conquer it, and thrive. What will self-care look like at the end of that scenario? When you have finished writing, rehearse your coping plan in your mind. Imagine that scenario playing out. For example, "I take my medication, I go to the family picnic, and I socialize with my aunt using DEAR MAN" (a set of skills that helps you navigate difficult interactions; see page 96). "Then I treat myself by going for a coffee at my favorite place."

continues >

How did you do in your imagined scenario? What happened? What did you learn? This exercise can bring up some uncomfortable feelings, so be sure to do something nice for yourself afterward.

PART 4

Embracing Your Coping Skills

No matter what your experience, it's important to remember that you are not powerless when it comes to bipolar disorder. In addition to the treatment you get from your doctor or therapist, there are many coping skills you can use to manage difficult emotions and stressors, reduce your symptoms, and stay on track.

In this section, you will explore which coping skills are and are not working for you in your life. You will explore some healthy strategies you can use, including emotional, social, spiritual, and other skills. You will also find practices you can use to help you when life feels overwhelming and skills to turn down the volume when life is a little too loud. My goal is to empower you with a range of positive coping skills to manage your moods as you move forward.

Exploring Your Coping Skills

What are your current go-to coping skills? I've listed some common ones here, and you can write in others that you typically use. Be honest with yourself; nobody will see this list but you.

Healthy coping skills

- [ ] Calling a friend
- [ ] Doing physical exercise
- [ ] Using mindfulness skills
- [ ] Doing breathing exercises
- [ ] Engaging in prayer, meditation, or spiritual practice
- [ ] Taking a brief vacation
- [ ] ____________________

Unhealthy coping skills

- [ ] Isolating from others
- [ ] Abusing alcohol and/or drugs
- [ ] Oversleeping
- [ ] Undersleeping
- [ ] Avoiding
- [ ] Procrastinating
- [ ] Spending impulsively
- [ ] Overeating
- [ ] Undereating
- [ ] Acting in anger or aggression
- [ ] ____________________

How did it go? Did you find you have more healthy coping skills or unhealthy ones? In the trackers on pages 118 and 119, you can keep track of the skills you use over two weeks to help you get a clearer picture of which skills you rely on the most. How are these coping skills working for you? Do they genuinely help you feel better and get more done, or are they just avoidance tactics?

Coping Skills for Depression

What are your current go-to coping skills when you are experiencing a depressive episode? Would you describe these coping skills as healthy? Would you describe these coping skills as helpful? What about these coping skills is currently most helpful for you? What is least helpful?

Coping Skills for Mania

What are your current go-to coping skills when you are experiencing a manic episode? Would you describe these coping skills as healthy? Would you describe these coping skills as helpful? What about these coping skills is currently most helpful for you? What is least helpful?

Comparing Your Skills

How similar are the coping skills you use when you're depressed versus when you're manic? How are they different? What types of coping skills bring you more relief? What types of skills do not bring you relief at all?

What's Worked Well

Think of a time in your life when you were struggling. How did you feel physically during that time? How did you feel mentally? How have you improved since then? What have you done to improve? What is different now? Write about how you have improved your life, and reflect on (and give yourself credit for!) your improvements.

A Closer Look at What Isn't Serving You

Take some time to think more about the coping skills you tend to rely on that are unhealthy. Where did you learn these? What about them is unhealthy? How do they affect your life in an unhealthy way?

Room for Improvement

What coping skills do you think you need to improve on? How would improving your coping skills reduce your suffering? How would improving your coping skills improve your quality of life?

A Time and a Place

When do you find you most need to use your coping skills? Is there a time of day when you are most distressed? Are there specific people you find you need to use coping skills around the most? Is there a place (work, the bus, the grocery store)? What different skills might be appropriate for different places?

Ground Yourself in Your Senses

Observing your surroundings using your five senses can help ground you when life feels chaotic or when anxiety builds. Spend a few minutes trying this simple exercise now so that you have some practice. Then, when you need it, it will be easier to do. Before you start, take some long, deep breaths to help move yourself to a calmer state. When you are ready, follow these steps, observing things you don't usually take notice of.

- Notice five things you can see.
- Notice four things you can feel.
- Notice three things you can hear.
- Notice two things you can smell.
- Notice one thing you can taste.

As you notice each of these things, simply observe them without judging or categorizing them. When you are finished, take note of how you feel. Do you feel calmer? More grounded? In what circumstances might this practice be helpful for you?

Social Support

Do you reach out to friends or peers when you find yourself struggling? How can social coping skills give you some relief? Do your friends or peers help turn down the noise when you are struggling with depression? Are your friends more helpful or harmful when you are struggling with a manic episode? How would you like your friends to be more supportive when you are struggling?

IMPROVE the Moment

IMPROVE the Moment is a group of coping skills that offer many short, helpful ways to reduce distress and improve your current situation. It is used in dialectical behavior therapy (DBT).

IMPROVE stands for **I**magery, **M**eaning, **P**rayer, **R**elaxation, **O**ne thing in the moment, **V**acation, and (self-)**E**ncouragement.

Imagery: The goal with this skill is to use your imagination to picture yourself in a tranquil, peaceful place to help you relax and feel calmer.

Meaning: The goal with this skill is to find meaning in painful events, rely on your spiritual values, or hold on to a spiritual value or meaning that will give you strength.

Prayer: This skill is meant to open your heart and mind to your higher power, give things over to your higher power, or ask for strength. If you do not consider yourself spiritual, you can direct your thoughts to something else, such as nature or your better self.

Relaxation: With this skill, you prioritize self-care and relaxing actions such as taking a warm bath, massaging your neck, practicing yoga, or breathing deeply.

One thing in the moment: This skill shifts your awareness to being mindful, centering yourself into the moment, and focusing your whole attention on just one thing that is present right now.

Vacation: Vacation means you take a brief break from things with the intention of returning later. To give yourself a brief vacation, you might take a nap, go for a drive, turn off your phone for the day, or take a one-hour break from work.

(self-)**E**ncouragement: With this skill, you stop criticizing yourself and become your own cheerleader with positive statements and affirmations such as "I can do this" and "I am doing my best right now."

Reflect on which of these you would like to explore and make a list of any ideas that come to mind.

Healthy Ways to Cope

Think about your current unhealthy coping skills when you become triggered and how they are serving—or not serving—you in your life. Make a list of your triggers. Then think about the unhealthy coping skill you use to deal with that trigger. In the next column, list an alternative, healthy coping skill you can use the next time you are triggered. I've added an example for you.

TRIGGERING FEELING, THOUGHT, OR EVENT	CURRENT UNHEALTHY COPING SKILL(S)	ALTERNATIVE HEALTHY COPING SKILL(S)
I feel really down on myself and like I don't want to see anyone.	*I turn off my phone and stay at home in bed all day so I don't have to speak with anyone.*	*I reach out to a friend or loved one and do something I enjoy with them.*

TRIGGERING FEELING, THOUGHT, OR EVENT	CURRENT UNHEALTHY COPING SKILL(S)	ALTERNATIVE HEALTHY COPING SKILL(S)

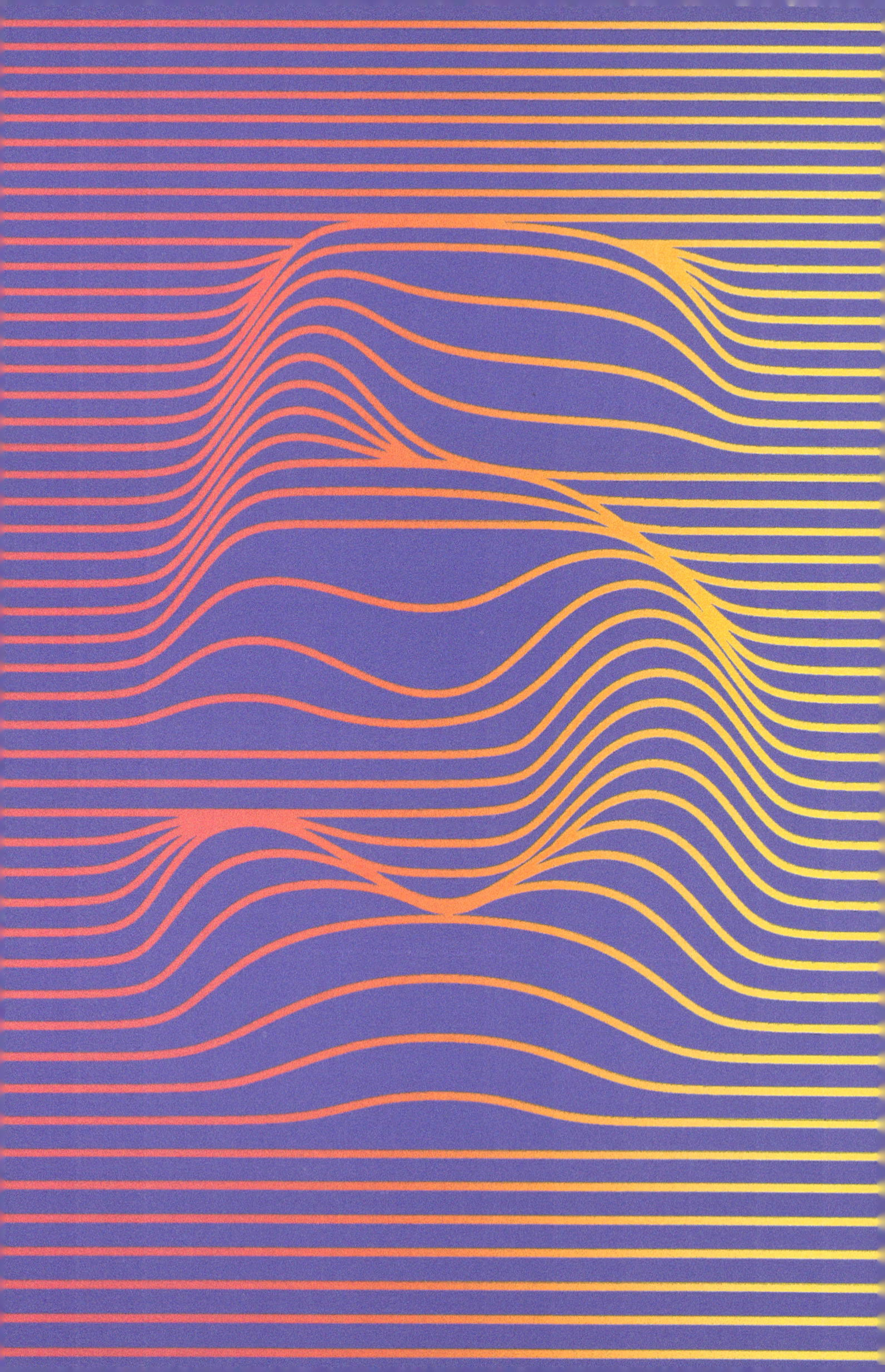

PART 5

Establishing Healthy Relationships

Relationships and support are fundamental parts of managing any mental health diagnosis. Having a solid support system to turn to during manic and depressive episodes will make a world of difference in how you get through your recovery process and on with your life. But relationships require a lot of work and a lot of give and take on everyone's part. One important aspect of healthy relationships is to establish firm boundaries as a way of making sure you protect yourself and your needs—and to respect the boundaries of others as well. Establishing a healthy relationship with yourself—knowing when to have grace with yourself and when to push yourself—is also vital for your recovery and well-being.

Your Support Systems

Who are currently your primary supports? How do these people support you? What about these relationships feels healthy? What about these relationships feels unhealthy? What happens in these relationships that tells you they are healthy or unhealthy? What can you do to improve these relationships—both the healthy and the unhealthy ones?

Reflecting on Past Relationships

In the past, what about your relationships has been a struggle? What has been a positive? Do you find yourself repeating the same patterns (good or bad) within relationships or gravitating toward the same type of people? What about your relationships would you like to improve?

continues >

Positive Bonds

Now think about the positive relationships in your life right now—be they with family, friends, coworkers, a partner, or otherwise. How do these relationships support your mental health? What about them is most helpful? How can you nurture these relationships and find more like them in the future?

Focusing on Your Priorities

In every relationship, there will be conflicts of one type or another. Focusing on what your priority is within that conflict will help you choose an endearment strategy that is more likely to get you the outcome you want. Your priority might be self-respect, preserving the relationship itself, doing what you feel is right, or something else. It's important to know what your priorities are when you're heading for a conflict so you don't let problems build; you know why you are engaging in the conflict, and you know what result or change you would like to see.

In this exercise, you will learn more about the three different types of priorities and how to plan for conversations you may need to have. As you read through each description, bring to mind a conflict—past, present, or hypothetical—in which the priority type reflects your desired outcome, and then answer the prompts.

Objectives: Your objective might be meeting a specific goal or attaining a certain outcome from an interaction. This focuses on the outcome or a change instead of feelings. Examples of objectives include standing up for something you think is right, getting your opinion across effectively, refusing an unwanted request, and asking for something in an effective way. These are goals-focused priorities. Now bring to mind a real or hypothetical interaction in which an objective is your specific priority, and fill in the following prompts.

My objective:

What I want to convey:

How I want to feel about myself:

What I want the other person to understand:

How I want the other person to feel about me:

continues >

Relationships: When your goal is strengthening or keeping a relationship, the relationship is the priority. An important question to ask yourself before engaging in a discussion with someone in which this is your main objective is "How do I want this person to feel about me?" This approach helps you strike a balance between your immediate goals and your long-term goal of keeping the relationship. Keep in mind that you do not want to preserve a relationship that is damaging in the long term. Now bring to mind a real or hypothetical interaction in which the relationship is your priority and fill in the following prompts.

The relationship I want to preserve or improve:

How I want to feel:

How I want the other person to feel:

Self-Respect: When you're acting from a place of self-respect, you are acting in a way that represents your morals and values. This might be standing up for what you believe in, defending a friend or family member, or doing the right thing even when it is not the popular thing. The key question to ask yourself here is "How do I want to feel about myself?" Now bring to mind a real or hypothetical interaction in which self-respect is your priority and answer the following prompts.

The morals and values I want to uphold: ______

How I want to feel about myself: ______

How I want the other person to feel about me: ______

Your Boundaries

Do you have a hard time setting boundaries within relationships? In what way(s) do you struggle with boundaries? Do you give too much of yourself within relationships? Do you have a hard time saying no within relationships? Do people tend to take advantage of you? How do these behaviors affect you? How do these behaviors affect your relationships?

The Effects of Past Relationships

How have past relationships gotten you in trouble? How have these relationships affected your mental health? What would you change about these relationships? How could better boundaries have affected the decisions you made in these relationships?

Saying No Gracefully

It's okay to say no to things you are not interested in or that you would prefer not to do. Sometimes you might feel compelled or pressured into doing things because your friends want to do them even when you don't feel comfortable or able to join them. Saying no is perfectly okay when you do it in a kind and genuine way, and it will not ruin a friendship.

The next time a friend or loved one asks you to do something you don't want to do, practice saying no without giving an apology or an excuse. Simply say, "No thanks, that does not sound fun tonight" or "No thank you, I'm not interested in that." You can also try suggesting another activity: "No thanks, but would you be interested in seeing ______________________?" or "No thanks, but would you like to go eat _______?"

Use this space to prepare what you would like to say in situations where you often feel compelled or pressured to do things, or write down what you wish you had said in the past when this happened.

Boundaries with Others

What boundaries do you set for others? These could be rules, limits, or expectations you set around your privacy, your right to change your mind, how you spend your time with others, or anything else you can think of. Are these boundaries too firm with some things and too porous with others?

Boundaries with Yourself

Now, write about the boundaries you set for yourself. These might be around your health, your bedtime, your social media use, how you spend your money, or anything else you can think of. Are there some you find harder than others to stick to?

New Boundaries

If you were to create some new boundaries in your life, what might they be? List them here. How could they benefit your relationships with others and yourself? How can you implement them?

DEAR MAN Coping Skill

The DEAR MAN skill teaches you how to be skillful in asking for what you need. Created by Marsha M. Linehan, the acronym stands for:

Describe the current situation.

Express your feelings about the situation using "I feel" statements.

Assert yourself by asking for what you want or need or by saying no to a request.

Reinforce the positive or negative consequences of the other person's behavior ahead of time.

(be) **M**indful of your goal—ignore attacks and repeat your requests or say no as if you are a broken record. There's no need to escalate the interaction.

Appear confident and effective, use a strong voice, and make eye contact.

Negotiate—be willing to give to get or problem-solve to get what you need.

Now, thinking of a difficult conversation you need to have or something you need to ask for, prepare a conversation in which you use the skills in DEAR MAN to help you navigate the interaction, remain calm, and be clear about what you would like to happen.

Describe:

Express:

Assert:

Reinforce:

(be) **M**indful:

Appear confident:

Negotiate:

Your Relationship with Yourself

How is your relationship with yourself? How do you talk to yourself? How do you think about yourself? Do you value yourself? Do you think you are worthy of good things? Do you respect yourself the way you respect other people?

Validation in Relationships

Validating yourself—accepting your thoughts, feelings, and internal experiences—can be a powerful skill. It doesn't mean you believe everything you say, do, and feel is justified, but it does mean letting in and being present with your thoughts, feelings, and internal experiences.

Validating others is also an important skill for starting and maintain healthy relationships. In this sense, "validation" means identifying and communicating your understanding of what another person is experiencing based on the information you get from their words and body language and from the context of the situation. Here are some ideas for ways you can validate yourself and others.

Validate Yourself

- Describe your emotions, experiences, and actions as facts.
- Accept hurts and ways people have tried to invalidate your feelings and experiences, and allow yourself to feel the pain.
- When you make mistakes, remember that you are human and humans regularly make mistakes.
- Speak to yourself with kindness and compassion, just as you would to a friend.
- Stand up for yourself and your thoughts. Don't put yourself and your beliefs down.
- When someone disagrees with you, be open to the idea of being wrong and learning from the experience.

Think of situations in which you may need validation.

Write a validation statement for yourself to practice when you make a mistake.

Write a validation statement for yourself to practice when you do something great.

continues >

Validate Others

- Give the other person your complete attention. Listen and observe mindfully and without judgment. Focus and make eye contact.
- Reflect back what you heard to demonstrate that you understand and that you are paying attention. Have an open mind and do not take offense if you are wrong.
- Be aware of what is not being said. Pay attention to the other person's body language, their face, what is happening around you, and what information you already have about the person. Look for the hidden messages.
- Try to understand the other person from their point of view.
- Acknowledge that you understand the other person's thoughts, beliefs, feelings, and actions given their current reality. Act as if all of those things are valid—because they are for that person. It doesn't mean you have to agree.
- Do not try to one-up the other person. Treat the other person as an equal, not as someone fragile or incapable—or powerful and inflexible. Let go of being defensive.

Think of situations in which others may need validation. Write your validating statement in response to each example.

It's Thursday night, and your friend calls you crying. She tells you that her boyfriend of eight months just broke up with her via text message.

Your coworker, with whom you typically eat lunch, tells you that her dog died and she is feeling very sad and lonely.

Who do you trust to talk about your experiences living with bipolar disorder? What do you think is important for them to know? What support and encouragement is valuable for you?

Different Kinds of Friendships

Do you find yourself gravitating toward different friend groups depending on your mood? Do you have a different friend group when you are manic than you do when you are experiencing a depressive episode? How does each friend group meet your needs emotionally? Is there anything unhealthy about these friendships that you would like to change?

Leaning into Vulnerability

When you are living with depression, anxiety, or difficult emotions, your instinct might be to hide away and avoid others. But opening up and being vulnerable with people you trust can help you overcome the isolation you feel and help you feel more grounded and supported. If you find it difficult to reach out to others, try this approach the next time you are struggling.

1. Reach out to a loved one whom you trust and ask them if you can confide in them about how you're feeling.
2. Ask them when would be a good time to talk. Doing this enables them to create time and space for you and not be caught off guard.
3. Ask if it would be easier if you sent them an email about what's going on and then they can call you back within a day or two. (Remember that just because they are not available to talk today does not mean they don't care. Some people are very busy, or they need to clear emotional space to be able to understand what you are going to tell them.)
4. Have the conversation with the person, sharing your feelings honestly with them.

Thinking about Self-Care

How frequently do you engage in self-care? What motivates you to engage in self-care? What does self-care look like for you? Do you do your self-care alone or with a group of people? Do you find yourself relaxed and renewed after doing something to take care of yourself, or does it feel like a chore? If it feels like a chore, what could you do differently?

Valuing Your Progress

Taking the time to acknowledge your achievements can be an act of self-care. Use this space to detail what you are most proud of about how you have carried yourself in your journey so far.

Lessons Learned

What have you learned about yourself using this journal so far? Is there anything that has surprised you? Have some things given you hope? Use this space to write about any insight you have gained and how it can help you in the future.

PART 6

Tracking Your Moods & Behaviors

In this section, you'll find a series of fourteen-day trackers that align with the first five sections in this book so you can track manic symptoms, depressive symptoms, triggers, coping skills, and healthy relationships. Each one lists the symptoms and/or behaviors associated with that topic with space to write anything else you wish to track that is specific to your experience. You may find it best to work with each tracker at a different time so that you track your moods and behaviors over ten weeks in total. However, you are free to use the trackers in whatever way works best for you.

It may be helpful to use the information or patterns you observe to avoid certain behaviors in the future to prevent triggers, manic episodes, or depressive episodes. If you are in therapy, you may find it useful to share this information with your therapist or psychiatrist as a means of figuring out your triggers and changes in mood. This information is meant to help you better understand your symptoms, mood changes, and triggers but not to be a diagnostic tool.

Tracking Manic Symptoms

Use these pages to track any symptoms of mania over a two-week period. I've listed the common symptoms here, but remember that symptoms can be different for each person. Check the boxes of

WEEK 1	SUN	MON	TUE	WED	THU	FRI	SAT
Increased energy							
Distractibility							
Impulsivity (spending, sex, drugs, etc.)							
Decreased sleep							
Elevated self-esteem							
Agitation/irritability							
Fast talking							
Racing thoughts							
Euphoria							
Other:							
Other:							
Other:							

any symptoms you experience each day. You can use the extra rows to write in your own symptoms to track.

WEEK 2	SUN	MON	TUE	WED	THU	FRI	SAT
Increased energy							
Distractibility							
Impulsivity (spending, sex, drugs, etc.)							
Decreased sleep							
Elevated self-esteem							
Agitation/irritability							
Fast talking							
Racing thoughts							
Euphoria							
Other:							
Other:							
Other:							

Tracking Depressive Symptoms

Use these pages to track any symptoms of depression over a two-week period. I've listed the common symptoms here, but remember that symptoms can be different for each person. Check the boxes

WEEK 1	SUN	MON	TUE	WED	THU	FRI	SAT
Loss of interest in activities							
Isolation							
Increased need for sleep							
Loss of appetite or increased appetite							
Fatigue							
Hopelessness							
Thoughts of suicide							
Feelings of emptiness							
Restlessness or irritability							
Other:							
Other:							
Other:							

of any symptoms you experience each day. You can use the extra rows to write in your own symptoms to track.

WEEK 2	SUN	MON	TUE	WED	THU	FRI	SAT
Loss of interest in activities							
Isolation							
Increased need for sleep							
Loss of appetite or increased appetite							
Fatigue							
Hopelessness							
Thoughts of suicide							
Feelings of emptiness							
Restlessness or irritability							
Other:							
Other:							
Other:							

Tracking Your Triggers

Use these pages to track your triggers over a two-week period. I've listed the common triggers here, but remember that triggers can be different for each person. Check the boxes of any symptoms you

WEEK 1	SUN	MON	TUE	WED	THU	FRI	SAT
Poor sleep							
Physical illness/pain							
Poor nutrition and hydration							
High anxiety or stress							
Arguing with others							
Lack of exercise							
Not taking prescribed medications							
Drug or alcohol use							
Seasonal changes							
Other:							
Other:							
Other:							

experience each day. You can use the extra rows to write in your own triggers to track. As you complete the tracker, notice how each trigger can affect your mood.

WEEK 2	SUN	MON	TUE	WED	THU	FRI	SAT
Poor sleep							
Physical illness/pain							
Poor nutrition and hydration							
High anxiety or stress							
Arguing with others							
Lack of exercise							
Not taking prescribed medications							
Drug or alcohol use							
Seasonal changes							
Other:							
Other:							
Other:							

Tracking Your Coping Skills

Use these pages to track your coping skills over a two-week period. I've listed the common coping skills here, but remember that each person finds the coping skills that work best for them. Check the boxes of any

WEEK 1	SUN	MON	TUE	WED	THU	FRI	SAT
Self-care activities							
Keeping in touch with loved ones							
Physical exercise							
Mindfulness skills							
Breathing exercises							
Good sleep							
Prayer or spiritual practice							
Taking a brief break							
Eating well and staying hydrated							
STOP skill							
IMPROVE the Moment							
Other:							
Other:							

skills you use each day. You can use the extra rows to write in other skills that you find helpful. As you complete the tracker, notice how using your coping skills helps you manage your moods.

WEEK 2	SUN	MON	TUE	WED	THU	FRI	SAT
Self-care activities							
Keeping in touch with loved ones							
Physical exercise							
Mindfulness skills							
Breathing exercises							
Good sleep							
Prayer or spiritual practice							
Taking a brief break							
Eating well and staying hydrated							
STOP skill							
IMPROVE the Moment							
Other:							
Other:							

Tracking Healthy Relationships

Use these pages to track how you use priorities, boundaries, and other relationship skills to have healthier relationships over a two-week period. I've listed the common boundary and relationship skills here, but remember that each person finds the skills that work best for them. Check the

WEEK 1	SUN	MON	TUE	WED	THU	FRI	SAT
Asking for help when I need it							
Saying no to something I didn't want to do							
Expressing my feelings in a calm way							
Respecting myself and my priorities							
Validating myself							
Validating others							
DEAR MAN							
Maintaining my boundaries							
Identifying priorities in a conflict							
Checking the facts							
Other:							
Other:							

boxes of any skills you use each day. You can use the extra rows to write in other skills that you find helpful. As you complete the tracker, notice how using your skills helps you improve and strengthen your relationships.

WEEK 2	SUN	MON	TUE	WED	THU	FRI	SAT
Asking for help when I need it							
Saying no to something I didn't want to do							
Expressing my feelings in a calm way							
Respecting myself and my priorities							
Validating myself							
Validating others							
DEAR MAN							
Maintaining my boundaries							
Identifying priorities in a conflict							
Checking the facts							
Other:							
Other:							

NAVIGATING THE ROAD AHEAD

Congratulations on completing this journey to better understanding and managing bipolar disorder! You've explored how your symptoms play a role in your life and your relationships and how to best cope with your bipolar disorder in your everyday life—and that's no easy task! Taking a deep dive into understanding your own mental health struggles can be challenging, and this was a brave first step.

My hope is that you found meaning, hope, and insight throughout the time you spent and the work you did with this journal. No matter where you are in your journey navigating bipolar disorder, please continue exploring all the resources available to you for healing, success and improvement. Best wishes for you and your mental health. Things will only continue to get better!

RESOURCES

Online Resources

Depression and Bipolar Support Alliance

DBSAlliance.org

This organization offers help and services, including support groups, to improve the lives of people who have mood disorders.

International Bipolar Foundation

IBPF.org

This organization offers information and resources for individuals and family members of those living with bipolar disorder.

National Institute of Mental Health

NIMH.nih.gov/health/topics/bipolar-disorder

This website contains information about bipolar disorder as well as treatment and therapy resources.

Substance Abuse and Mental Health Services Administration (SAMHSA)

SAMHSA.gov/find-help/treatment

The SAMHSA website includes information and resources for those living with bipolar disorder, including a locator map for treatment services.

Books

The Bipolar Disorder Survival Guide: What You and Your Family Need to Know (3rd edition), by David J. Miklowitz, Guilford Press, 2019

Bipolar II Disorder Workbook: Managing Recurring Depression, Hypomania, and Anxiety, by Stephanie McMurrich Roberts, Louisa Grandin Sylvia, and Noreen A. Reilly-Harrington, New Harbinger Publications, 2014

A Mood Apart: The Thinker's Guide to Emotion and Its Disorders, by Peter C. Whybrow, William Morrow, 1998

Take Charge of Bipolar Disorder: A 4-Step Plan for You and Your Loved Ones to Manage the Illness and Create Lasting Stability, by Julie A. Fast and John Preston, Warner Wellness, 2006

This War within My Mind, by John Poehler, based on the blog *The Bipolar Battle*, 2020

REFERENCES

Harvard Medical School. "Shining a Light on Winter Depression." Harvard Health Publishing. November 1, 2019. health.harvard .edu/mind-and-mood/shining-a-light-on-winter-depression.

Liebson, Elizabeth. "Can Light Therapies Help with Bipolar Disorder?" Harvard Health Publishing. February 18, 2020. health .harvard.edu/blog/can-light-therapies-help-with-bipolar -disorder-2020021818901.

Linehan, Marsha M. *DBT Skills Training Manual*. New York: Guilford Press, 2014.

ABOUT THE AUTHOR

Whitney Frost, LPC, MA, is a licensed professional counselor in Denver, Colorado, where she owns a private practice focusing on women who are navigating the struggles of borderline personality disorder, bipolar disorder, infertility, and perinatal and postpartum mood disorders. Whitney's practice focuses on providing quality mental health care to women in the greater Denver area regardless of their ability to pay. Whitney is a mother of two and enjoys spending time with her family and volunteering in her free time.

www.ingramcontent.com/pod-product-compliance
Lightning Source LLC
Jackson TN
JSHW061018190325
80860JS00002B/14

* 9 7 8 1 6 3 8 7 8 4 5 2 4 *